In-Between Things

Priscilla Tey

Candlewick Press

An **in-between** thing is a thing in the middle.

The cat is **between** the table that's green and the chair with the tear, sitting right over there.

The dog is **between** the floor and the cat (and does not enjoy being in the middle like that!).

The chair is **between** the parrot and carpet.
The carpet is **between** the floor and the chair.

What will you find **between** the floor and the carpet?

Yuck!

A fur ball, a dust ball, and a nasty clump of hair!

But it doesn't stop there!

Between the floor and the ground below,

lies a world of **in-between** things to show.

Pick any two things to look **in between.**

Look left and look right; there's much to be seen!

An **in-between** thing can
separate two things,
which is sometimes a helpful
and necessary thing.

The glass **in between**
keeps fish wet and us dry.
It separates the cat from
that tasty-looking guy.

If you build a fort and fill it with light,

it will separate you from the monsters at night.

If you travel outside
and then back in once more,
an **in-between** thing
you will need is a door.
Doors take you through walls
separating kitchens from halls,

and you from
that pie filled with
scrumptious meatballs.

In-between things can
transport you somewhere,
take you to places, from here . . .

to over there.

You can walk down the **in-between** coal-colored street
that's **in between** this house and the house that has feet.

And if you meet an **in-between**

stream or a creek,

cross an **in-between** bridge
for dry paws and dry feet.

Some spaces **between** places can stretch very far.

Don't walk all those paces! Take a train or a car.

Take a little bit of this
and a little bit of that,
and an **in-between** thing
is the mix that you'll get.

Take a little bit of yellow and
a little bit of blue,
and the **in-between** color
is a new greenish hue.

When a bit of wet rain
hits a bit of dry sand,
the mud feels sticky
and damp on your hand!

A little bit of skirt and
a little bit of short,
and the **in-between**
outfit you get is a skort.

A little bit of spoon
and a little bit of fork,
and the **in-between**
tool you get is a spork.

If you dance a little jiggy
and add a little wiggle,
your **in-between** jiggle
will make everyone giggle.

For an **in-between** thing,
no matter how absurd,
there is always some form
of an **in-between** word,

Between
"oink" and "meow,"
you might hear
Moink-Kee-Ow;

between a cow and zebra . . .

MOINK
MOINK

you'd have a **zebrow**.

If you thought up a thing
between a giraffe
and a poodle,
you could create a poofy
and spotted **giroodle**.

Not quite this and not that,
in-between things aren't clear yet.

The sky is dim—
neither dark nor light.
Is it sunrise or sunset?
Is it daybreak or night?

Are you out in the cold
or too close to hot?
Or are you warm in
that **in-between** spot?

Look around for **in-between** things to scribble.

Try making yourself the thing in the middle.

Keep looking, eyes open, and

in-between things will come clear.

All kinds of wacky and weird will appear.

Search and explore every cranny and nook,

around the world, in your head . . .

and **between** the two covers of this
In-Between Things book!

For Judy,
and Spider and Jaycee

First edition 2018

Library of Congress Catalog Card Number pending
ISBN 978-0-7636-8983-4

18 19 20 21 22 23 LEO 10 9 8 7 6 5 4 3 2 1

Printed in Heshan, Guangdong, China

This book was typeset in Univers and Clarendon.
The illustrations were done in mixed media.

Candlewick Press
99 Dover Street
Somerville, Massachusetts 02144

visit us at www.candlewick.com